THE DEVIL ON WHEELS

by GORDON IRVING

From *"Going Down Hill on a Bicycle"*

"With lifted feet, hand still,
I am poised, and down the hill
Dart, with heedful mind;
The air goes by in a wind.

Swifter, and yet more swift,
Till the heart, with a mighty lift,
Makes the lungs laugh, the throat cry;
'O bird, see; see, bird I fly...'

Speed slackens now, I float
Awhile in my airy boat;
Till when the wheels scarce crawl,
My feet to the treadles fall.

Alas, that the longest hill
Must end in a vale; but still,
Who climbs with toil, whereso'er,
Shall find wings waiting there."

THE DEVIL ON WHEELS

by GORDON IRVING

The Story of
Kirkpatrick Macmillan
Inventor of the Bicycle

Illustrations by
Thomas M. Taylor

Alloway Publishing

© GORDON IRVING

First Published in 1986
by
Alloway Publishing Ltd.,
24 Beresford Terrace, Ayr.

Printed in Scotland
by
Walker & Connell Ltd.,
Hastings Square, Darvel,
Ayrshire.

ISBN 0-907526-25-X

By the same Author:

GREAT SCOT! (Sir Harry Lauder biography)

THE GOOD AULD DAYS
(Story of Scotland's Entertainers from Music-Hall to Television)

THE WIT OF THE SCOTS

THE WIT OF ROBERT BURNS

THE SOLWAY SMUGGLERS

THE FIRST 200 YEARS
(Story of Dumfries and Galloway Royal Infirmary)

BRUSH UP YOUR SCOTLAND!

ANNIE LAURIE (Story of the Song)

TAKE NO NOTICE! (World's Funniest Signs)

TAKE NO MORE NOTICE (More Funny Signs)

THE BEN LINE

CONDITIONS OF SALE

FOREWORD

Inventor — *"A man with wheels in his head."* — Anon.

In the writing of this biography of Kirkpatrick Macmillan, a Scotsman too little honoured among his ain folk, I am indebted to a host of people stretching from southern Scotland to Australia who have passed on valuable information about my subject. A great deal of it, hitherto unpublished, has been in danger of passing out of living memory.

All of four decades ago the first original research on Macmillan appeared in a successful little book of the same title, published, appropriately, in the town of Dumfries by the well-remembered firm of Robert Dinwiddie. (Whisper it, that book, now almost out of print, sold for the unbelievable sum of half-a-crown!).

Now that original story of mine has been added to, extended, and fully updated, and my wish is that this new biography will do justice to a Scotsman whose name is not as well-known as it ought to be. Even schoolboys in Scotland are not told the true-life story of one of their countrymen. The bicycle is still very much in use, more so in the villages and towns of southern England, and its popularity surely proves that, even in this technological age, we must still keep our faith and trust in simple things.

It was a simple idea first thought of in a rural corner of Britain in 1839, and I feel Macmillan's story is well worth the telling for the interest — and, dare I say it, also the entertainment! — of both young people and their elders.

As the plaque on the wall of his cottage home puts it, "He builded better than he knew." How true!

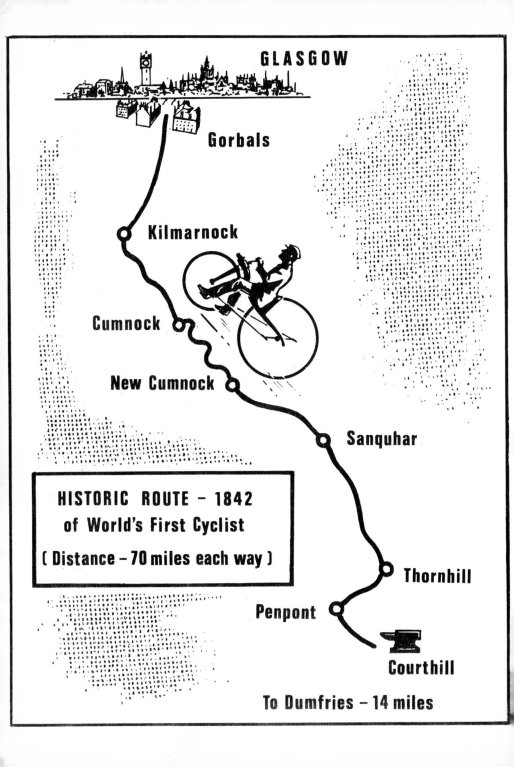

KIRKPATRICK MACMILLAN
(from an old sketch)

CONTENTS

IN THE BEGINNING

Not so long ago an experiment was tried out in Boston, in the USA. Cyclists, motorists and subway commuters took part.

Five groups, each comprising a cyclist, a motorist and a subway traveller, set off at different times during the day, leaving an appointed point and making for Boston City Hall.

And guess what? In every instance it was the cyclist who arrived at the destination first.

I have no axe to grind in favour of cyclists, even though in the following pages I will be telling of the first man in the world to travel on a pedal-propelled machine, but I'm sure there is a moral somewhere in that tale from Boston. A moral for all of us in an age when petrol costs so much and yet a humble bicycle can take us here, there and most places without costing a penny.

But to my story, a romantic one, I hope.... concerning a man who was born in a quiet South of Scotland village in the year 1813. His name — Kirkpatrick Macmillan.

I find it difficult to understand why Scots folk, and more especially those of Dumfriesshire origin, should tend to forget it was one of their own kith and kin who actually invented the first pedal bicycle.

Until 1892 it was the general belief that the first man to apply driving gear to two wheels was Gavin Dalzell, a cooper from Lesmahagow, in Lanarkshire, and indeed Dalzell's descendants claimed that honour for him until then.

But on April 16 1892 Gavin Dalzell's son wrote a letter to Mr James Johnstone, of the Glasgow Cycling Club.

It ran as follows:-

"Dear Mr Johnstone,
As the result of the enquiries you have made into the question of the earliest inventor of the bicycle or geared dandy-horse, I have no hesitation in frankly admitting that you have proved that Kirkpatrick Macmillan constructed his one before my father constructed his.

Yours very truly,
(Signed) J. B. Dalzell.

It appears that Mr Johnstone, after considerable research and questioning of the older residents of Dumfriesshire, had proved that Dalzell's bicycle dated only to 1846-47, and that Macmillan

had made his at least six or seven years previously.

His main piece of evidence was an account of one John Leslie, blacksmith, Lesmahâgow, against Gavin Dalzell for "putting on ironwork on bicycle." This account was dated the 27th of January and 10th of February, 1847.

My own extensive researches have uncovered much of the intriguing story of the rural blacksmith's son who devised the idea of putting pedal propulsion to the old-style "dandy-horse" or velocipede, and who was laughed to scorn when he rode it from the village smithy at Courthill, in the parish of Keir, to Glasgow, in June 1842.

The young lad from the country, faced with curious and sometimes rowdy citizens as he entered Glasgow, had the misfortune to knock over a small girl, and, on being hauled before the magistrates, was fined five shillings for speeding — at eight miles an hour!

The first man in the world, I'd dare to say, who was ever punished for going too fast on the highway.

But of that true and engrossing chapter in his life I'll tell more in due course.

Until Macmillan from Scotland got his idea, people used to ride up and down the rough lanes and roads of Britain astride wooden "hobby-horses" — pieces of wood, with wheels, pushing themselves along with foot-power. It was left for the blacksmith's son to devise his two-wheeled machine operated with a drive of treadles to the rear wheel.

Macmillan's home was close to the Duke of Buccleuch's estate at Drumlanrig Castle, in a lovely unspoiled area of south-west Scotland.

In fact, after a few years working with his father Robert Macmillan, he was offered a job in the Duke's own smithy on the estate.

The story goes — and I have no reason to doubt it, having gathered it from different sources — that one day the young Macmillan chanced to see a "hobby-horse" which belonged to a local wood-turner named Charteris.

The contrivance at once interested the keen and youthful blacksmith, for he was of a inventive turn of kind, and had already saved himself a lot of labour by fixing a pedal and crank to his smithy grindstone.

But he realised that to propel the hobby-horse was a task calling for much labour. The rider had to keep pushing hard with his feet on the ground. Anyone who has ever tried to ride along on an old-fashioned scooter knows the work entailed.

Macmillan was convinced that he could change things by building a velocipede that would move by — wonder of wonders — mechanical means.

He mentioned his dream of an idea to some neighbours, and their reaction was immediate — and positive. They laughed. "You're daft, laddie!" they said. "Daft."

The young Scotsman was determined to prove them wrong.

DON'T LAUGH AT "PATE"

I hardly think you can blame Scotsmen — or the world — for not honouring or even remembering Kirkpatrick Macmillan, blacksmith and bicycle inventor. The man himself did not fully realise the importance of his work.

It was not, in fact, until the end of the 19th century that the true inventor of the pedal bicycle was proclaimed as the Dumfriesshire blacksmith.

Macmillan, or, as he was known among his friends and neighbours "Daft Pate", appears to have been an unusually interesting and even offbeat character, but there is, strangely, very little contemporary evidence of his career.

Possibly in some old yellowing newspaper files there may yet lie several undiscovered pieces of information that would throw light on one or two doubtful points. But, on the whole, references to the blacksmith from Keir Mill, in Dumfriesshire, are few and difficult to find.

Until some years ago Macmillan was still a living memory in the Penpont and Keir districts, and much valuable information could be gleaned from the memories of several old people then alive.

I myself spent some weeks travelling around the district — on a bicycle, I must aptly add — and succeeded in eliciting many interesting facts and anecdotes about the inventor.

Then I struck it lucky, but not in Scotland. A message from a police inspector in Liverpool gave me the intriguing news that Kirkpatrick Macmillan's only son, John, was then still alive, and living as a resident in the Belmont Road Public Assistance Institution.

He had moved there by choice, for, as a former policeman in the Merseyside city, he knew the warden well, liked the home, and, moreover, he was an excellent sharpener of knives, a trait and skill he had inherited from his boyhood days in the village smithy.

For many years John Macmillan was a popular policeman in Liverpool, and as he approached his 80s, he expressed a wish to take up his abode in the home. It was there I found him, and drew from him some fascinating information about his father, his family and the world's first pedal bicycle.

The memories of son John are quite detailed, and I plan to spell them out in a later chapter in this book.

I think it has got to be remembered that Kirkpatrick Macmillan, a son of the soil, grew up in a localised, stern and sturdy tradition, and knew few of the amenities and benefits of life as it was developing in the larger towns and big cities of 19th century Scotland.

The remarkable thing is that, by sheer dint of his own unflinching purpose, he has given to the world an invention that has held its own since first it appeared on those rocky dusty Lowland Scottish roads around 1839 and 1840.

The bicycle is today found in every country, and is used by many people who still shun the motor-car — from crofters and farming folk to elegant ladies in Sussex villages, from kings and queens and princes to Africans in their developing homelands. In fact, a bicycle is the dream of many a young black African, as letters to pen pals in Britain have so often revealed.

There are few boys and girls who have not, at some stage in their growing careers, achieved the never-to-be-forgotten pleasure of becoming proud owners of this simple means of travel.

On the lanes and roads of the world, from China to Peru, from Prestwick to Pretoria, you will find the pedal bicycle.

Housewives do their shopping awheel. Business-men, anxious to stay slim and fit, ride to offices and warehouse astride a bicycle.

In the dawn hours, in any part of the world where industry abounds, you will encounter workers cycling steadily to mill or factory. Despite the ease and speed of motor transport, the humble bike is still in demand.

Over on the Continent of Europe the bicycle is twice as popular as it is in England, Scotland, Ireland or Wales. Almost every second person owns his or her own machine, and uses it regularly on the level roads of Holland, France, Denmark and Belgium.

Someone has said that "the man who invented the bicycle deserves the thanks of humanity."

That man, oddly enough, is not a household name. Like so many other inventors — from the steam engine to penicillin, from pneumatic tyres to television — he was a Scotsman.

Don't laugh, like his contemporaries, at poor "Daft Pate" (short for "Kirkpatrick") Macmillan. But laugh, I ask you, at his entertaining life and adventures, the subject and raw material of this biography.

"GO TO WORK ON A BIKE"

People in many countries have reason to say "thank-you" to the blacksmith Macmillan for his bright idea of putting pedal propulsion to the old-style hobby-horse.

They all enjoy riding a bike, and the high cost of petrol is not the only reason. Pedal travel makes us healthier.

More than seventy million Americans now ride bicycles, and sales alone in the U.S.A. have risen by 35 per cent.

Traffic experts agree that queues of cars, bumper to bumper, must be eliminated, sooner or later. The bicycle could be the answer.

Dr. Ralph Galen, a dentist in Cambridge, Massachusetts, cycles 12 miles to his surgery every day of the year — except in the worst of winter weather.

Eugene A. Sloane, public relations director of the Midwest Stock Exchange, was making a daily 25-mile trip from his Evanston, Illinois, home to his Chicago office on a multi-speed lightweight bicycle, and that in his mid-50s.

Traffic observers see bicycle commuting as the coming trend for a growing percentage of the community.

Once you're in town, you can get around faster, they point out.

It is no harder to ride a bike than it is to walk, but it goes four or five times as fast, and it goes downhill by itself even without leg-power to shove it.

Scotland's bicycle pioneer, blacksmith Macmillan, truly "builded better than he knew."

For the average commuter the bicycle can cut down dramatically in costs.

"You don't put petrol into a bicycle," one said, "and you don't shell out pounds in servicing or in road tax."

In fact, experts in New York claim that, if only ten per cent of car commuters were to switch to bicycles, that city's traffic congestion would be solved immediately.

"Bike commuter paths" are being planned for some cities. And one idea being put forward in industry is that companies could set up what might be termed "bicycle lending libraries." Company cars would be out, and employees at all levels could borrow a bike from their firm and use it for getting to work.

Holland and Denmark already show Britain the way in the use of the bicycle. Copenhagen is packed with cyclists; thousands of them sweep out from the city every evening, hardly causing a traffic jam.

Many roads in Britain, away from the frightening motorways, are regarded as very suitable for bicycle riding. There are not too many hills, and commuting by bicycle could become a pleasant way of visiting friends, shopping or going to work.

Cycling is being increasingly recognised as an effective yet fun way to stay in shape.

You slim down, your legs grow lean and strong, and you enjoy the method of travel.

Macmillan from Dumfriesshire knew a good thing when he tackled it. "Daft Pate" was not the mad blacksmith he was made out to be, as my continuing story will tell.

A BOY AND AN IDEA

Mr and Mrs Robert Macmillan and their five children had their home in a little whitewashed cottage in the rolling countryside of Dumfriesshire, in southern Scotland. It was the early part of last century, and new ideas were in the air as a rural world developed.

It was an era so different from today. Life was real, life was simple. Roads were poor or almost non-existent. Nobody had even dreamt of fast motorways, for the simple reason that there were no motor-cars.

Railway trains were starting to make their bow, and letters were taken from town to town by mail-coaches, pulled by horses.

Kirkpatrick was the youngest of the Macmillan family, and he loved to romp around his father's blacksmith's "shop" or smithy, with his older brothers John and George and Walter, and to play with his little sister Mary.

It was largely a farming community, and cattle and sheep and horses were the mainstay of the area. The sturdy horses that the farmers brought to the Macmillan smithy to be "shoe-ed" were a considerable attraction for little Pate, as the boy was nicknamed by a contraction of Kirkpatrick, spoken in a strong Dumfriesshire lilt.

Sometimes the boy would help his father at the grindstone or the anvil, for he was fascinated by wheels and handles, cranks and iron bars.

It would be one afternoon around the year 1820 when young Kirkpatrick ran into his parents with exciting news.

"I've been talking to the old men at Thornhill Cross," he said. "They tell us lots of things are happening up in Glasgow.

"People are moving about more, and lots of bright new ideas are being talked about. They say you maybe won't have to go by the railways or the stage-coaches all the time. And there's a new thing called the 'hobby-horse,' a bit of wood with wheels, and it moves along when you push."

The young Macmillan boy seemed enthralled by tales told by the travellers as the coaches changed horses on their run between Glasgow and Carlisle.

He was becoming a bit of a dreamer, of course, and he kept asking himself what anyone could do to think up some new machine that would let a boy or a girl, a man or a woman, move along the country roads — quickly and easily.

It was a simple enough life in the Scotland of 1820 when our 'Pate' was only seven. But a hard one compared with today, almost two centuries later.

In the morning, on the stroke of five o'clock, his mother would waken him, cook a steaming bowl of porridge and milk, and get the lad to his lessons.

Young Kirkpatrick was not a bookish type. "I dinna want to live with reading and writing a' my life!" he would say. "Aye, books are a' very well for John and George and Walter. But I like horses too much. I want to grow up and be a blacksmith like my faither."

Pieces of iron and wood interested the youngster far more than books of grammar and arithmetic.

He learned how to plough the fields, and to milk cows, and sow seed, and reap corn. At night he pottered about the smithy, learning as much as he could about ploughs and pumps and other bits of mechanical things.

Across the little River Scaur, not far from his home, lived the farmer and his wife at Morton Holm. Robert Macmillan arranged that his youngest lad, so agriculture-minded, should start work there.

"Aye, you're richt, Robert," the farmer told the blacksmith one day, "this lad of yours is real keen on horses. He seems to understand their ways.... he's got a winning way with the animals."

The news pleased Robert Macmillan and his wife Mary. Their other boys were going up to Glasgow to learn academic things at the university. They were pleased that 'Pate' was content to stay a country laddie.

Then, one day, a rich gentleman who lived near the village of Holywood, near Dumfries, heard about the blacksmith's boy.

"How would you like to be my coachman?" he asked 'Pate,' who by now was seventeen. "I'd want you to break in my horses, and try them out on the flat and in jumps."

It wasn't a job every lad would have taken on. But 'Pate' the teenager was tall and strong, and, what's more, by now he really knew the ways of horses. He was kind and patient by nature.

Before many more months had passed, 'Pate' had made quite a name for himself by breaking-in and training the wildest of the

Dumfriesshire horses. He loved to tame a horse down, then yolk it to a gig or carriage, and gently try it out on the road.

It was, however, a different kind of "horse" that was to be so much part of his future. An iron "horse."

EUREKA!

His work as groom and coachman was, I'm certain, the start of it all.

Macmillan was starting to get the confident feel of driving along on the open road.

As he moved out from the narrow confines of the smithy and the farm to train a frisky horse on the highway, such as it was, he got to know the drivers of the stage-coaches going up and down from Glasgow.

"Hey there, young fellow!" they would shout to him, "That's a bonnie animal you've got there. He's ridin' well today."

And there and then the stage-coach men would pace young 'Pate' for miles past the village of Holywood, and north to Thornhill and beyond.

As the years went by and experience came his way, Macmillan grew into a handsome lad of 22, a clever and compassionate coachman. He got the feel of being a travelling type, but he didn't forget his parents and family at the Courthill smithy, and often he would be called in to help out when the farmers brought in lots of horses to be shod.

Like the bright and ambitious person he was, Macmillan was keen to make progress. He listened to everyone, and would regularly walk over to the Wallyford smithy on the Duke of Buccleuch's Drumlanrig Castle estate and chat with the blacksmith there.

One day, excitedly, 'Pate' burst in on his mother and father at the Courthill cottage. "Faither," he said, "There's just the job for me now. The Duke needs a new blacksmith, and guess what, I've been offered the job.

"Mind you, only an apprentice at the moment, but over the weeks I'll learn. It's a grand chance."

At the Duke of Buccleuch's smithy 'Pate' became popular. One of the other apprentices there was John Findlater. 'Pate' and John became good friends.

Then it happened — the event that was to change his life. On a fine Springtime morning he went to repair a farmer's plough near the village of Carronbridge.

It was an ordinary errand and a very mundane sort of job, but the results of the young blacksmith's trip that day were soon, it turned out, to go echoing round the world.

'Pate' told what he had seen when he met up with John Findlater that evening back at the Duke's smithy.

"Great...a great idea!" he said, recovering his breath. "Saw it with my verra own eyes. I did. On the road to Carronbridge!

"Man, John, it was great. Just a simple strut of wood, with two bits of a wheel.

"See, you sit astride it, push with your feet on the road, and then you scoot — aye, scoot — yourself along.

"The man tells me his machine is a 'hobby-horse.' Aye, some call it a dandy-horse. Och, John lad, it moves in great style."

John Findlater nodded and smiled. At that moment an idea must have come to them both in a flash.

"Right we'll make one!" they both exclaimed, at one and the same time.

There and then 'Pate' Macmillan and John Findlater shook hands on the bargain, closed up the Duke of Buccleuch's smithy for the night, and went home to think about — the new hobby horse.

Over the next few weeks and months the two young blacksmiths kept themselves busy, building their new form of transport.

'Pate' took his rough machine home to add some finishing touches at his father's smithy, and his parents smiled with just a touch of sympathetic compassion.

"Sorry, son," said Robert Macmillan, "but you'll never ride on a piece of wood like that! Stick to the old-fashioned horse and cart. It's not worth all the trouble of pushing it — that is, if you can manage to propel yoursel on it at all!"

But the young Macmillan and his friend John were not to be put off. After a few more weeks they had their contraption ready for the road.

One warm June evening 'Pate' tried out the district's first hobby-horse. An inquisitive crowd gathered round the smithy door.

As the lad moved off, a scornful cheer went up.

"Och, the laddie's daft!" said old Sam Maxwell, from the village. "Daft Pate. Silly silly lad. Naebody ever moved on two wheels before."

But old Sam Maxwell, despite his years of experience, was wrong.

The 24-year-old blacksmith's son went creaking and cranking down the country road while his family and neighbours waited in suspense, expecting to see him run into the nearest ditch.

Kirkpatrick swirled and criss-crossed the road on his home-made hobby-horse. But he kept his balance and went scooting on his way.

Three weeks later John Findlater put the final touches to his own dandy-horse, and together the two blacksmiths rode along the country lanes when their day's work was done.

Still, it was the hills and the inclines that worried Macmillan. This hobby-horse idea was fine for level terrain, but you soon tired of pushing with your feet on the ground.

And, as for those hills, well, there was nothing for it but to dismount and walk.

"Surely," 'Pate' said to himself, "surely some new kind of 'horse' can be built that will propel itself and its rider, and you won't have to make your feet touch the ground."

At night, in bed, he would lie for hours just thinking about it. The idea must be so simple. Yet nobody had devised it... well, not yet.

"Y'know, it can be done," he told his work-mate John. "Nothing should be impossible in this new age of ours. Things are changing, and we've got to make them change with us."

Whispers began that something was about to happen at the Courthill smithy.

In fact, there was a minor sensation, rural style, in the district when the word got around that a completely new type of machine was slowly taking shape in the tiny workshop at Robert Macmillan's home.

Young 'Pate', they said, was trying to build a machine, a devilish machine, that would actually move along the road with a man on it — and all the rider needed to do was to push some bits of wood back and forward, to and fro, and the thing would balance itself.

The villagers, not sympathetic to innovation, smirked, scoffed and laughed at the very idea.

"But naebody has ever done it, and naebody ever will," they cried.

Macmillan continued with his project, carrying wood and iron into the smithy. Each evening the neighbours, passing the door, could hear him hard at work.

It was a rural revolution in miniature, and the result had to come out.

For inside that workshop, at this quiet smithy cottage in the Lowlands of Scotland, the world's first pedal-bicycle was slowly taking shape.

O MEIN PAPA!

The son of the bicycle inventor, the late Mr John Macmillan, was 76 and living modestly in a poor-law institution in Liverpool when I made contact with him around the year 1940. His memories were many. They were also happy ones.

John Macmillan, one-time policeman in Liverpool, was then the only remaining direct link with the inventor, for his sister Mary had died in 1928 in Bournemouth.

One thing that made him chuckle was to realise that cyclists in the middle of the 20th century were planning to reconstruct his father's famous ride to Glasgow of June 1842.

His father, he said, would have been greatly amused at the idea, and would only have hoped that the cyclists of 1939 (just as the Hitler war-clouds were gathering) would not be mistaken for the Devil on Wheels, as his father had been a full century before.

John Macmillan's personal reminiscences of early days at the Courthill Smithy were graphic enough, so much so that I propose to quote in this chapter the best of them. Despite long absence from Dumfriesshire, his memories were clear.

"On the kitchen shelf at Courthill," he recalled, "there stood a big bottle something like those seen inside the windows of sweet shops.

"When my father died, this bottle was within an inch off the top of being filled with teeth that he had pulled, for he acted as local dentist as well as blacksmith in his day.

"The teeth in the bottle didn't represent one-quarter of those he had drawn, for people used to take those he had pulled away with them.

"He used to lance the gum first before pulling the tooth, and gas, of course, was unknown in those days.

"I remember when he pulled out a tooth for me, I was very young at the time, perhaps about nine or ten years old.

"My jaw was very sore, and my Aunt Ann, who was housekeeper to my father, decided that I should have it out, so I had to submit.

"I remember a woman bringing in a little girl with the toothache. My father spoke to her in the usual crooning way he had with children, and, hiding the forceps under his fingers, he pretended to feel for the sore tooth.

"Before she had time to say 'Jack Robinson,' the tooth was out. I thought at the time that it was very quick and smart on his part.

"The only time my father ever charged for pulling out a tooth was when he wanted a new pair of forceps. He never charged for bleeding or doctoring horses or cattle, nor when any of the neighbours wanted the loan of his pony and gig.

"Another time, I remember, a man and woman brought a little girl in who had pushed a piece of slate pencil up her nostril. Neither of them could get it out.

"She had hardly sat down when my father showed them the pencil in his hand.

"He had nothing there but the pencil, and the parents were greatly amused. They kept feeling the child's nose to see if the pencil was still there.

John Macmillan was only fifteen years of age when his father died in 1878, and he left Scotland shortly afterwards.

He saw his father only once on a bicycle — rather significant.

"And," said son John, "he did not appear to ride it very well. The reason, I suppose, was that the pedals were on the front wheel, the machine not being rear-driven like his own velocipede."

About a year or so before his father died, John remembered a local gentleman bringing a penny-farthing bicycle to the smithy to get some small repairs.

"The front wheel was about five feet high, with a solid rubber tyre in a grooved rim.

"There was a steep incline in front of the smithy, and when my father was away, I got this bicycle out and took it to the top of the incline.

"With the aid of a milestone there, I got mounted and started off, with my feet, of course, not near the pedals.

"I got on very well until I reached the bottom of the incline, but when I tried to get down, the machine took a sudden turn and went into the gutter at the side.

"The farthing wheel seemed to come up all of a sudden behind me, and I went over the handlebars, head first, into a thorn hedge.

"When I got out, my hands and head were a sight with blood. I think my father suspected how I got all scratched, but he didn't ask any questions. That was the first and only time that I rode a penny-farthing bicycle."

Kirkpatrick Macmillan's mother saw to the education of the older members of her family, and, as 'Pate' was one of the youngest, he got only the 'scrapings' of the pot. It was his boast that he acquired most of his education by attending a night-school when he was thirty years of age.

His son remembered one unusual feature about his father — his laugh.

"He seemed to hiss through his teeth instead of laughing aloud in the manner of most people. It was something like the hissing of a groom when he is grooming his horse, and I suppose he retained that laugh from the time he was a coachman.

"He was a dab hand at making things for the farming community among whom he lived.

"For instance, he made two ploughs different from the ordinary plough.

"One he showed at the big Highland Show at Dumfries. I remember finding a card among my father's effects, and on it were printed the words 'Macmillan's Plough Without a Screw.'

"The other plough he made shortly before he died, and he used to say that it 'could be taken to pieces and put in a kirk.' He sold it to a farmer in Dumfriesshire, and it may be there yet.

"My father also made some agricultural implements for William Ewart Gladstone, who was then Chancellor of the Exchequer, and was complimented for his fine work. He was very proud of this, and often used to mention it.

"There were no veterinary surgeons within miles of Courthill, and the result was that, if anything ailed either the neighbours' horses or cattle, dogs or cats, they sent immediately for my father.

"Bleeding, either by leech or lance, was the fashion in those days.

"First of all my father used to fasten a belt round the bottom of the horse's neck, drawing it very tight.

"On the near and left side of the neck there is a small swirl of hair, and underneath is a vein or artery. My father had a lance in his left hand, and a small wooden mallet in his right.

"Feeling for the vein with his finger, he would place the lance on top and strike a blow with the mallet.

"I had to stand close by holding a bucket to catch the blood when it spurted out.

"My father took two or three pints from the animal, and then, with an ordinary pin, fastened the wound up again. He next pulled a couple of strands from the horses' tail and tied them round each end of the pin. The horses didn't seem to feel any pain, and the only sign of feeling they gave was when my father struck the lance with the mallet, and they threw up their heads."

John Macmillan remembered how his father was always "a very quick worker," and said it was remarkable how quickly he fashioned any article he was making, large or small.

"When he was delivering one blow with the hammer, he always seemed to know where he would strike with the next.

"I once saw him make eight pairs of horse shoes in an hour, and not a hair turned in doing it.

"Another day when he was going to a funeral I saw him throw off his leather apron, go upstairs, and in ten minutes he returned shaved, washed and dressed in his black clothes and top hat.

"He was also a devout Christian. With my sister Mary and myself, he walked to Virginhall Free Church where we sat on the last seat in the gallery. My father and mother attended the Moody and Sankey meetings when they were held in the neighbourhood. Whenever the weather was bad or the Scaur overflowed its banks, he would take down the book, and each of us would read a chapter."

Macmillan, according to his son, was very bitter against drink and tobacco. He used to give the smithy apprentices a couple of shillings or half-a-crown if they would stop smoking.

A lasting boyhood memory: "One day he asked me for a bit of slate pencil, and putting my hand in my waistcoat pocket, I handed him a piece. When he had finished with it, he put it in his mouth, and I think I can see the expression on his face — he had tasted the tobacco on the pencil. He made a grab at me and chased me out of the smithy, calling me a lazy good-for-nothing and telling me to go and hire for the harvest.

"I took him at his word, went ot the Cross at Thornhill, and hired myself to a local farmer!"

A BIKE IS BORN

Inside the tiny smithy at Courthill, sited unobtrusively by the roadside in the quiet green lowlands of southern Scotland, the world's first pedal-driven bicycle was taking shape. Slowly but surely.

By today's comparisons it was, of course, a quaint and awkward-looking contrivance, and at first glance you would have said nobody would ever sit astride and move on so cumbersome a vehicle. But it had pedals and cranks, and it was the first that man had ever made.

It is a fine tribute to the craftsmanship and ingenuity of the humble country blacksmith, a trade now hard to find, that such an epoch-making machine should have been invented and built in a little hamlet so far from the madding crowd.

The country folk came from all over Dumfriesshire and neighbouring Kirkcudbrightshire to catch a view of young 'Pate' Macmillan's contraption. And they had to admit it was cleverly contrived. Whether a man could travel on it or not remained to be seen.

Its wheels were made of wood, and it had iron-band tyres shrunk on to them after beating.

It had a frame which consisted of a wooden bar, forked to embrace the rear driving-wheel and carrying axle bearings near its end.

Its inventor, like all "mad" inventors, had great faith in his idea. His new "horse" was to be driven by cranks on the rear wheel, and these in turn would be revolved by swinging rods operated by horizontally rocking pedals.

Propulsion was, in fact, not unlike that of the steam locomotive on the railways.

Macmillan's steering wheel was carried in an iron fork, and the pivot passed through the frame with the handlebars attached above.

The saddle was mounted on a spring bolted to the frame, and was at such a height that, as in modern bicycles, the feet of the rider could be easily placed on the ground.

So proud was Kirkpatrick of his invention that he devised an adornment, a carved representation of a horse's head at the front end of the frame. It was, so he felt, a handsome piece of workmanship, and even the scoffers felt it had all the hallmarks of good craftmanship about it.

But the 64,000-dollar question was — would it work? That was the question everybody, even 'Pate' himself, was asking.

The villagers and neighbours in the hamlet of Keir Mill still had their doubts.

"The laddie will never ride this devilish thing!" they said. "It's impossible. He's oot o' his heid."

Fortunately, Macmillan, a dreamer and a idealist, was not to be discouraged. His friend and colleague Findlater gave moral support.

The two rural Scots had visions of a brave new world where one day every person, no matter how rich or poor, would have a velocipede with pedals to ride along the highways in all hemi-spheres.

Getting down to reality, Macmillan decided that it would be useful to travel quickly.

So, to secure a greater speed on his machine, he made his rear wheel 40 inches in diameter, and his front about 32 inches. This would allow for a higher "gear".

The major worry concerned the weight of the contraption. It weighed almost 57 lbs., and it was obvious that it would require a strong rider and an energetic leg thrust to handle it.

By autumn 1839 Macmillan had completed the building of his machine. It had taken him more than twelve months to make, but he was confident of its capabilites, and he made up his mind to show the world how good and useful it would be.

*   *   *

Scores of interested spectators gathered that September evening when 'Pate' first wheeled his "devilish" machine out of the smithy workshop to try it on the road to Keir.

I wish I had been around in that country parish that day when it all started to happen. The village community gazed with suspicion as the young man led his velocipede out on to the roadway and began the difficult job of mounting it.

It was no easy task, but, luckily, Macmillan was tall and strong. He had to be to cope with the weight and the dead-centre effect of the horizontal backwards-and-forwards motion of the heavy pedals.

To get it started, he found it easier — until the cranks on his rear-driven wheel began to move at a fair speed — to mount his machine and get it going by striking the ground with his feet.

It was hard on his boots, but that was purely an incidental problem and one that would soon be solved.

There were cries of fear and even horror from the assembled country-folk when the inventor mounted his steed and started to push himself slowly down the road to Keir Mill.

The cries went up: "He'll never mak' it!", "The laddie's richt daft!", "Puir daft lad!", "Imagine it, a man ridin' on a pair o' wheels!"

So, down that Dumfriesshire road, creaked the world's first pedal bicycle, and, yes, the blacksmith's boy was actually bestriding it and getting it to move.

The villagers watched in total amazement as he lifted his feet to the pedals and went whizzing down the rough highway, the first person anywhere in the world to ride on a velocipede, and propel himself along without touching the ground.

The bicycle as we know it today had been born.

"DUMMY" RUN

"Ach, you'll be as daft as yon young Pate ower at Courthill, aye thinkin' o' somethin' new . . . and crazy!"

The expression was heard regularly in the pleasant farming country of southern Scotland as friends and neighbours discussed the "devilish" machine which the young son of the Courthill blacksmith ˙ was building. News of Macmillan's unusual veolocipede spread through the district, and even into England beyond Gretna.

Kirkpatrick tried himself out regularly on the country roads.

In fact, many a ploughman and cottager, walking home of an evening, would be startled out of his senses as 'Pate' came trundling round a corner of a country lane in the gloaming.

It didn't take long for the epithet "daft" to stick to the young Scot, and a favourite expression at the Thornhill Fair, or at a village gathering, was: "Ach, lad, ye're as daft as daft Pate frae Courthill!"

Macmillan made a number of minor improvements to his contraption, and by the spring of 1840 he had struck on the idea of having a variable gear by putting several holes in the swinging levers hanging from the head of his steed.

Thus, by changing the length of the lever, he was able to shorten or lengthen the stroke, and so vary the power applied.

It must, indeed, have been an exhilarating experience for Kirkpatrick to pedal his mount furiously up and down the rough roadways of southern Scotland in those first few weeks and months after he had completed the building.

For he was — and few realised it — to be the first man in the world to prove that a human being could propel himself along on two wheels.

This riding a bicycle was a fascinating "lark", he discovered.

As a recreation in the evenings it was difficult to surpass. If machines like this could be contructed at a cheap cost, there was no knowing how far the sport might go.

Then, to secure greater ease and speed in getting up motion — the weight of the machine was immense — the inventor hit on the idea of fixing spikes to his boots to provide the rider with a firmer push-off from the ground.

This made him appear, for all the world, like the speedway racer of modern times.

*   *   *

Gradually, 'Pate' tried out longer runs. He went as far as Carronbridge in the north, at the entrance to the Dalveen Pass, and as far south as Holywood, where he had worked as a lad.

It wasn't long before he was trying out the longer run to Dumfires.

There were purchases to be made for his father in the thriving market town on the River Nith, and the douce townsfolk of Dumfries soon became familiar with the tall young blacksmith on his wooden contrivance.

By the autumn of 1840 he had become so adept at using his velocipede that he could complete the 14-mile journey to Dumfries inside 60 minutes. Not bad going fo: the world's pioneer cyclist!

It was about this time that a bright ne' idea came to him. Why not, he suddenly thought, why r ɔt show off his invention to the grand citizens in the city of Glasgow, so 70 miles away?

Why not, indeed? It was a daring thought for the age, but 'Pate' was convinced he could manage the feat. It would need plenty of preliminary preparation and training, he would have to be 100 per cent fit, but it was an opportunity that could not be missed.

Kirkpatrick had three brothers who lived in Glasgow, where they had risen to good positions.

His brother John, who had tutored the famous John Bright, was Classics master in Glasgow High School after seven years of teaching Latin and Greek to the scholars of Dumfries Academy.

George, another brother, was second master at Hutchesons' Grammar School, and a third was a clerk in a Glasgow warehouse.

All three had the advantage of a good education and had risen in the world far beyond the status of young 'Pate', who had to be content with the life of a rural blacksmith.

The inventor was determined to show his brothers —
and the people of Glasgow, too — that he had ideas and an
invention which might, one day, benefit the entire human
race.

Besides, the 26-year-old countryman had high hopes of
selling his invention to some far-seeing business man in the
city.

*   *   *

Secretly, quietly, the project was hatched out.
Macmillan hadn't the courage to mention it around Keir, for
he had experienced enough rebuffs in the last three years.

Better, he felt, to go ahead slowly with his preparations
and tell only his boon companion, John Findlater.

Practice makes perfect, they say, and to show the
people in his own district how simple and safe his velocipede
really was, he would often ride along the rural roads with a
child perched on his shoulder.

Little Elizabeth Fingland, the daughter of one of the
Drumlanrig estate workers, with whom he had lodged while
acting as an apprentice to the Duke's chief blacksmith, was
one of the youngsters so honoured.

Many an evening Elizabeth would go sailing down the
road from the smithy at Drumlanrig Mains to the Castle,
perched on his shoulders while the inventor held her firmly
with his left hand and steered with the other.

At other times Macmillan would ride over to the nearby
village of Moniaive in the evenings and visit his sister,
Isabella.

These short trips around the district were excellent
practice for his bigger project.

'Pate' had heard from the drivers of the Glasgow stage
coaches of the route he would have to take.

It would be, they said, to the north-west, through
Sanquhar and the Cumnocks and Kilmarnock, and a gey
rough road full of pot-holes at that!

Naturally, pre-planning came into it. Macmillan could
not hope to make the trip inside one day, so he arranged with
a friend of his brother's university days — one John
McKinnell, parish schoolmaster at Old Cumnock — to put
him up for the night and break his journey there.

* * *

The summer of 1841 was not favourable for his venture. It was a season of stormy weather, wind and rain, and, in any case, there was enough work at the Courthill smithy, where he now assisted his father, to keep him fully occupied until the winter. The trip would have to wait until the summer of 1842.

In May of that year Macmillan broached a mention of his project to his family. They were aghast at the idea.

To travel all the way to Glasgow and back on a pair of wheels without any protective covering, and alone at that, was a thing no man in his senses would ever attempt, they said.

"Dinna do it, son!" said his father. "It'll be the very death o' you, and we've had enough tragedy in the family without adding another.

"Besides, they'll no reckon you're human when and if you ride intae Glasgow. They'll hae you hanged on the gallows for trying out sic a devilish bit o' machinery!"

Young Kirkpatrick had much respect for his parents, and he did not usually disregard their advice, but on this occasion his mind was made up.

He realised that he must do something to popularise his worthy steed before the summer was out.

The big city of Glasgow was only seventy miles away, and, besides, the call of the open road was too much. He was resolved to go through with the attempt.

THE DE'IL'S AWA' . . .

Summer time in the green and pleasant Lowlands of Scotland, and it is twenty-five minutes past the hour of seven on the historic evening of June the sixth, 1842.

Again, I wish I had been born in that era, ready to witness a piece of history on the open road.

The place: the tiny 'smithy on the roadway between Keir Mill and Penpont. A group of countrymen and women are gathering . . . and chattering.

Something is happening inside Robert Macmillan's workshop. The laddie 'Pate', fast becoming a grown man, is up to another of his famous ploys.

The news gets around, and at first nobody will believe it. The young son of the 'smithy is actually getting his velocipede ready for a trip on wheels to the city on the Clyde.

A cheer, half of encouragement, half of derision, goes up from the crowd as the tall young blacksmith wheels out his contrivance and gets it ready for the high road.

Daft Pate Macmillan is preparing for his pioneer ride from Courthill to Glasgow.

Robert and Mary Macmillan, his parents, are too frightened to say anything. They can only stand and watch their son in sheer amazement.

Several of the older neighbours push forward to give him cautious words of advice. Others try to dissuade him from making the devilish trip.

But 'Pate's' mind is made up. John McKinnell will be waiting for him that night in the parish schoolhouse at Old Cumnock, and he has already sent a letter on by mail coach to his brothers in the city, notifying them of his intended arrival. The inventor is ready for the road.

* * *

The old clock in the 'smithy strikes eight as Pate mounts his wooden machine and rides off northwards towards Penpont. The onlookers give him a final half-hearted cheer as he disappears from sight down the roadway.

Meanwhile, ahead of the intrepid blacksmith, news of his ride spreads. Cottage folks come out in the June dusk to see him approaching in a cloud of dust.

Mothers, it has been recorded, called their children indoors. A man was coming along the highway from the south on a pair of wheels, they said, and the likes of it had never been seen before. It might well be the very devil himself!

This was, indeed, history in the making, and yet nobody appreciated it.

Slowly the miles sped by. By now 'Pate' was making a comfortable speed of seven miles an hour, and the world's first bicyclist was riding his 57 lbs. contrivance through Sanquhar and Kirkconnel and northwards towards Old Cumnock.

Darkness came on, and belated country people walking to their farms and cottages were caught unawares by the approaching traveller on wheels. What more natural than they should take to their heels in fright and scurry as quickly as they could into the safety of their homes.

"Aye, it's the verra De'il himsel'," was the cry as mothers plucked their offspring to bosoms and hurried "ben the hoose".

Meanwhile, in the schoolhouse in Old Cumnock, John McKinnell was waiting anxiously for his guest. He was late.

Eleven o'clock struck, and still no sign of his approach. Weren't all decent Scots folk in their beds long since!

Schoolmaster McKinnell began to grow uneasy. Something must have happened en route to his young blacksmith friend from the south.

Maybe he had been the victim of his own daring and had spilled himself into a roadside ditch, of which there were so many.

Or maybe some angry villagers had mobbed him on the journey. More likely still, this strange contrivance on which he rode had maybe broken down on the way.

Midnight, and still no sign of young Macmillan's approach. John McKinnell began to get anxious.

Outside the air was cool, and a bright moon shone down from a summer sky. McKinnell took a walk outside his home and paced up and down, peering into the distance for a glimpse of the expected travelling guest on two wheels.

* * *

At the other end of the township, down McKinlay's Brae, a young man from Old Cumnock was making his way homeward on foot. He was James Kennedy, a local shoemaker, and he was whistling happily to himself, for he had just seen his sweetheart, Jean Vallance, home to her mother's cottage outside the village. Things were going nicely with their love romance.

Jean was a bonnie Ayrshire lass, one of the prettiest in the district, and they were planning to wed in the parish kirk in a few month's time.

The moon rode high above, sentinel-like, in a perfect sky. Not a sound broke the silence. Life so far from the confines of the city was an ideal life, thought young Kennedy to himself; nothing here to disturb the even tenor of their ways.

A creaking sound in the distance halted him suddenly in his track. He tried hard to think what it might be. A midnight thief, maybe, breaking into a poultry-run.

The sound came nearer. It was like the jangle of iron on the roadway. A strange mysterious sort of clatter — he had never heard the like before.

James Kennedy steeled himself and looked round. It was then he saw it!

At the top of the brae, a tall, dark apparition, almost like a man, was travelling slowly down towards him — and, of all things, by God, on a pair of wheels!

It needed no strong impetus for the young shoemaker to decide what his next step would be.

Struck with horror and fright at the crazy thing racing towards him, Kennedy took to his heels, leaped over the nearest dyke, and ran for his life across the fields to the village.

I'm sure Kirkpatrick Macmillan, inventor and cyclist, little knew of the fear and trepidation he had struck in the young fellow from the Cumnock.

He was tired after his evening's journey, and he had not counted on being so late in reaching his schoolmaster friend in Ayrshire.

At full speed he pedalled down McKinlay's Brae at twenty minutes past the midnight hour, and drew up with a screech outside the schoolhouse.

McKinnell was happy to see him and, despite the lateness of the hour, welcomed him to his fireside with open arms.

He was greatly interested in the young inventor and his velocipede, and for hours they talked into the night about the contraption and its capabilities. 'Pate' told many stories of its construction. It was well into the early morning when they finally retired to bed.

I'm sure our Dumfriesshire blacksmith slept soundly. It had been a fatiguing day over bumpy roads, but nearly half his journey was over. And hadn't he come half way to proving that the pedal bicycle could be used for long-distance travel?

JUNE 1842 — A 'MIRACLE' IN THE GORBALS

Macmillan's ride from Cumnock via Kilmarnock and into the south side of Glasgow is, without doubt, the most colourful part of an already colourful story.

It was, indeed, a 19th-century 'Miracle' in the Gorbals as this country lad pedalled his way into the rapidly-growing city and dumbfounded its residents, who thought they had already seen everything.

Even his ride through the town of Kilmarnock was epoch-making.

In fact, to quote "Tam Samson's Elegy" by Robert Burns, the good folk of the Ayrshire town might well ask: "Has auld Kilmarnock seen the De'il?"

The historic day was Tuesday, June the 7th, 1842. Perfect morning sunshine had greeted 'Pate' as he wakened from his few hours' slumber in the little schoolhouse bedroom in Cumnock. This was going to be a day of days.

After breakfast, John McKinnell said he would like to see his friend riding his steed in the village street. He had not had an opportunity to see it properly the previous night.

Macmillan readily agreed to this suggestion. He was the proud young man that day, and he must not miss this chance to show off his invention to so respected a friend as the schoolmaster of Old Cumnock.

So, out into the street he wheeled the cumbersome machine, and within a matter of minutes the usual interested gathering of spectators had congregated, wide-eyed and amazed.

What, they asked, what was this tall, good-looking young man going to do next?

Further up the street, inside the local shoemaker's establishment, young James Kennedy was flabbergasting his workmates with a strange and fantastic yarn.

He had, he said, been seeing Jean Vallance home the night before, and on his way back an apparition had appeared at the top of McKinlay's Brae — a man, yes, a man on a pair of wheels.

"Ach, dinna be daft James!" his workmates told him.

"You're ower much in love, that's whit's wrang wi' you! The moon must ha'e turned your mind. You've been seein' things!"

But Kennedy stuck to his story. "I tell you, I saw it wi' ma ain eyes!" he said. "There was nothin' the matter with ma senses. At the top o' the Brae it was, A tell you — a man on twa wheels."

But of course, nobody believed him.

"Think again, James," they said. "Think again, or you'll no' be in a fit state tae ha'e that weddin' of yours in August!"

Suddenly the sound of voices came from without. Something odd and offbeat was happening in the street below.

Rushing to the window, the shoemaking apprentices saw a sight which made them think again. A man . . . yes, a man was actually riding a contraption on wheels down the village street.

"There you are!" laughed Kennedy. "So what did I tell you! Now you'll be believin' me, I suppose."

*   *   *

But time was passing, the sun was rising high in the sky and Macmillan must pursue his journey to the city.

Ninety minutes later — on the stroke of ten o'clock — he bade good-bye to John McKinnell, thanked him for his hospitality, and prepared to depart.

He decided to give one last exhibition before he left, rode back on his track out of the village to the south, and climbed the incline to McKinlay's Brae, which he had descended with such frightening results on the previous night.

One man who was among the hundred or so to watch him ride down the Brae said afterwards:

"I saw this blacksmith lad do what I have never seen another do since, except in a circus.

"Yes, standing on the saddle and guiding the front wheel with his hand, he came down McKinlay's Brae at full speed . . . faster than man has ever done before. Man, it was a wonderful sight!"

As he finally rode out from Old Cumnock, Macmillan was given a great send-off. Practically everyone who lived in the village seemed to be there to see him commence the second stage of his journey.

For a mile and more beyond, the village school-children followed the rider on the strange machine. They were intrigued with the contrivance — no wonder, they had never seen the like before.

As Macmillan slowly covered the miles towards the city, he began to find the state of the roads better than they had been further south.

True, there were still holes and ruts and more holes, and the surface was not at all good for riding a velocipede along - particularly the world's first velocipede — but then, the highway did improve and he pursued his way at a steady eight miles per hour.

Women and children cheered him. Others — many others — still ran indoors when they saw him approaching. Workers in the fields left their crops to line the roadsides and see this amazing, this amusing "man on wheels" pass by.

By mid-day the sun had reached its peak and shone down on the fields and roads — a good augury for the inventor's pilgrimage, but the heat was almost stifling. Macmillan, sweating as he propelled the heavy piece of wood and iron, decided to call at a wayside cottage and beg a glass of milk.

A middle-aged woman came to the door in response to his knock. She took one look at the inventor, another at his machine, and then, closing the door hurriedly, exclaimed: "Na, na, ma mannie! You'll be a scissors-to-grind man, and A've nae wark for you the day!"

By early afternoon Macmillan had reached the outskirts of a busy market town. He stopped to ask his precise location and was told by a braver soul than usual: "Aye, laddie, aye, you're juist comin' in tae the toon o' Kilmarnock."

To Macmillan, who had never been further from home than Dumfries, there seemed to be hundreds of citizens in the Ayrshire town. Every person who mattered and who didn't matter appeared to have come out to see him.

Many were the cries of awe, wonder and surprise as he creaked on through the street.

Said one man to his neighbour: "Weel, A'll be damned, dae you see whit A see, Jock? Look — ower there, comin' through that crood o' folk there! It canna be . . . aye, but it is! A man, aye, a man, and he's run awa' wi' pairt o' an . . . pairt o' an engine!"

Half an hour later Macmillan had left Kilmarnock well behind him, and already in the distance he could catch a glimpse of the outskirts of a city. It looked strange to him, an innocent young countryman from the south; but this, he thought, this must be the place he had heard so much about — the grand business city of Glasgow.

He came in by the south side. Everywhere more and more crowds gathered to see him. News had spread like wildfire of his impending arrival, and the whole city of Glasgow seemed to have come out to greet him with wild guffaws and hurrahs.

In Gorbals that summer afternoon a miracle appeared to have occurred. Never before in the history of the city had the streets and pavements been so packed with people.

They had all come out to see this Scottish "Devil on Wheels!"

Confusion, of course, ensued, and young Pate did not know what to do to escape the melee. This unruly mob either wanted to throw him off his invention or to run him out of the town.

At half-past five an incident occurred. It was no fault of Macmillan's. So dense had the throng become and so loud the babble of voices that he decided to avoid it at one point, and to get away from the crowd he veered his mount round to ride along the pavement.

A little girl, aged five, ran out from a nearby close, and — even on a contrivance much lighter that his own — Macmillan could scarce have missed hitting her.

Skilfully wheeling, he just grazed her leg; but the little lass was so terror-stricken at the strange sight that she fell crying to the ground. Her leg was not injured, but the crowd thought otherwise.

They mobbed and clustered round the young countryman — so much, in fact, that a number of constables were quick to reach the scene and halt the inventor in his track.

"Catch him! Catch him!" called the bailies, and Macmillan was seized by the hands of the law. Already the little girl had completely recovered, and the mob was more interested in catching a glimpse of Pate's wonder horse than in seeing justice done.

But the law thought differently, it seemed. Full particulars were taken of the inventor's name and home address, his machine was taken into custody, and he himself was led off to the nearby police station.

Here his arrival — and particularly the advent of his "bicycle" — caused a great stir. Police and other officials crowded round the worried-looking visitor from the south.

He had scared a little girl out of her wits, they agreed. To go even further, in fact, he scared not only her but themselves as well, and investigation must be made into the matter.

It was the first case of its kind in Glasgow. To put it even more strongly, it was the first case of its kind in the world. This young Macmillan fellow, thought the police, must be formally charged with obstruction of the Queen's highway.

So they put his velocipede under lock and key, then led the inventor himself away and left him in a cell.

Macmillan was more than ashamed. For a God-fearing man as he was to fall into the clutches of the law, and to be locked up in the big city of Glasgow, was the most derogatory thing that could have happened!

"But, gentlemen," he protested, "I have done nothing wrong. I was only coming into Glasgow to show my piece of workmanship to my three brothers. My contrivance is quite harmless, I can assure you."

But the police would have none of it — at least until Pate summoned up sufficient courage to mention that two of his brothers occupied sound positions of authority in the city and that one of them, George, a school-master in Hutchesons' Grammar School, lived not so very far away.

A police constable was sent to bring George Macmillan to the station the while Kirkpatrick waited in his cell, growing more shamefaced as every minute passed. What a dishonour he had done his family by landing up in this amazing situation, he thought to himself.

By 7.30 that evening George Macmillan arrived. He came hurrying into the station with an officer of the law, immediately recognised his brother, learned of the plight he was in — and produced the necessary money to have the young man bailed out.

Only the velocipede spent that night in a Gorbals cell. It was a safe lodging-house for the world's first pedal cycle.

The two Macmillan brothers went home until next morning, when Pate was under an obligation to return to the Gorbals Public Bar and be legally charged in court with obstructing the passage.

He did not sleep much that night, despite many reassurances from his brothers that everything would be all right. He had invented a new method of propulsion, but he had also fallen into the hands of the magistrates. And that, for a respectable young blacksmith from the south of Scotland, would never be forgotten by the village folk at home!

FINED FOR "SPEEDING"

It was a court-room scene that would not have disgraced the best of comedy, in theatre or on television. One of the first persons in the world to be accused of driving dangerously, even speeding.

The setting was the public court in the Gorbals of Glasgow, a district on the south side of the Clyde city. The man in the dock — Kirkpatrick Macmillan, blacksmith, of Courthill smithy, in the hamlet of Keir Mill, near Penpont, Dumfriesshire.

The charge — riding to the danger of the populace, and knocking down a little Glasgow girl.

This was, indeed, history in the making as the court officer bawled: "Silence in Court", and the public benches quickly stilled to an unaccustomed silence as the tall young blacksmith who looked not unlike America's Abraham Lincoln sat nervously and self-consciously awaiting his trial.

The magistrate looked unusually stern, at least in the eyes of the countryman from Dumfriesshire. He also looked more than slightly nonplussed as he peered down at the man in the box.

The Clerk of the Court rose. "Your Honour", he began, "this is the charge. 'Kirkpatrick Macmillan, blacksmith, residing at Courthill, in the parish of Keir, in the county of Dumfries, is charged with having, on June 7, 1842, ridden along the pavement on a velocipede in the Barony of Gorbals to the obstruction of the passage, and with having, by so doing, thrown over a child.' "

The magistrate's face was a picture, his expression changing from surpirse and curiosity to wonderment, almost disbelief. Here was something he had never heard before.

"Mr Clerk of Court", he interrupted — "Mr Clerk, you state that the accused in this instance is charged with riding along the pavement — on a *velocipede!*"

"Yes, your Honour", replied the Clerk. "On a velocipede. For your Honour's information, this is a kind of modern-day hobby-horse, propelled by pedals and cranks.

"The accused, a humble countryman, owns one of these contraptions and is an expert at riding it. In fact, he is

understood to be the man who not only built it, but also *invented* it.

"It appears, your Honour, at least from what he has stated to us, that yesterday he came all the way from Old Cumnock in Ayrshire, a distance of forty miles, bestriding this . . . this velocipede, and that he performed that journey in the space of five hours . . ."

The magistrate showed even more amazement at this.

"Forty miles in five hours", he said, bemused. "No, I can't believe it! Eight miles an hour, and you say that he actually rode the machine under his own power.

"No, indeed, this modern craving for speed is something to be deplored, I must say. A man riding a machine of two wheels and making it progress without having to touch the ground. I just can't believe it."

The Clerk of the Court explained: "But, your Honour, it is perfectly correct. We have the contraption to prove it.

"You see, your Honour, it moves on two wheels, turned by means of a crank. Though, if I may say so, to make it progress appears to call for more labour than will be compensated for by the increase of speed.

"Incidentally, your Honour, the machine is meantime in the yard of this Court, and is available for inspection if you so desire."

The magistrate was still perplexed, stroked his chin, shook his head several times in disbelief, and then looked sternly at the man in the dock.

"My good fellow," he said, "you, Macmillan, must know as well as the rest of us that we simply can't have things like this going on. Eight miles an hour . . . why, that's simply not done. What's more, it's indecent!"

Kirkpatrick — "Daft Pate" — seemed in a state of shock, and was too ashamed to speak up.

The magistrate continued with his musing:

"Let me see, now. You state that this man from Dumfriesshire met with an accident in the Barony of Gorbals, and that he had the mishap to knock down a little girl in the confusion, on a pavement, following his arrival in the city outskirts."

"That is correct, Your Honour," said the Clerk of Court, noting that by now the full story of the 'Miracle in the Gorbals' seemed to be getting through to the bench.

But the magistrate was obviously at a loss to know just what decision to take.

Again he stroked his chin, shook his head several times, then:

"If the accused will realise, this is a most unusual case, and I am indeed sorry to see you in this plight, Macmillan.

"But justice must be done. We cannot have young men speeding on the roads of Scotland (or of England, for that matter) in this style. The highways of this country will soon not be safe to travel on!

"Let me see, now. (Looking at notes). Yes, this does seem to be the first case of its kind. The very first.

"In fact, if it comes to that, it is also the first pedal-driven velocipede of its kind, too!

(Pause for thought) "I fine you, Macmillan — I fine you in the sum of five shillings. And never let it happen again.

"Oh, by the way, young man, if you are available at the end of this sitting, I would . . . I would like to view this devilish contraption of yours. . . .Yes, it just might be interesting to see how it really works."

*   *   *

Macmillan was relieved, greatly so, in fact, at the comparatively small extent of the fine, and readily agreed to let this bemused and rather stunned Glasgow magistrate have a close-up inspection of the machine afterwards in the yard behind the Court.

So it was that, half-an-hour later, a small group of Court officials joined Macmillan and the Gorbals magistrate on an informal inspection of the world's first pedal bicycle.

It caused Macmillan to smile again. The law and officialdom, he realised, were no longer frowning on the invention. They were revealing a keen interest in it at last.

*   *   *

It didn't take the inventor long to prove to the pompous little city magistrate that everything was in order — and very much so.

The latter looked in wonder at the "devilish" machine. "Wonderful! Amazing!" he said.

"And you tell us that you came all the way from the county of Dumfries on that piece of wood, under your very own feet propulsion? I can scarcely believe it."

"You may believe it or not as you wish, your Honour," said Pate. "But it's perfectly correct, I tell you. This is the first pedal velocipede in the country today, and I think I can claim the honour of having built it."

There and then, and with a touch of unaccustomed bravado, Macmillan mounted his special and very precious machine, got it into motion in the small and confined Court yard, and started to show how skilfully he could manoeuvre it. The onlookers were more than impressed.

The display over, Macmillan dismounted and awaited the verdict.

"Truly wonderful!" said the magistrate. "I congratulate you, Macmillan."

"Daft Pate" thanked him for the compliment. "Your Honour, the folk at home said I was out of my mind when I first made it. Now they should think otherwise, I hope."

"I am certain they will," said an approving magistrate. "The whole world will thank you for this invention, so, as a small tribute to your ingenuity, would you kindly permit me to grant you a favour..

"Here is the sum of money I have just fined you.

"Please take it from me as a small token of thanks for your invention.

"You have done something here that will deserve the appreciation of many generations to come — and the thanks, I am certain, of all humanity."

THE DEVIL" — AND AFTER

Anyone doing something new is bound to be talked about. So it was with Macmillan, blacksmith, now a sensation on two wheels.

His ride into the southern environs of Glasgow was already being recorded for the history books. The public prints of 1842 had to take notice of him.

Legend has it — and I would like to believe this! — that the street vendors of the time were already calling attention to the city's newspapers by shouting, to all and sundry: "Devil on Wheels! Devil on Wheels! The Devil comes to Glasgow riding on a Hobby-Horse!"

What is a fact is that the great city public were being induced to "read all about it" in their newspapers. It was almost as if, today, flying-saucers had landed on a city's parklands and were disgorging their occupants.

Anyhow, Jock Citizen of dear old Glasgow town was already buying his paper, reading the remarkable report — and coming to realise that a new and worthwhile machine had arrived on the earth.

According to one of the reports, it seemed that a gentleman who "stated he had come from near Thornhill, in Dumfriesshire, had been placed at the Gorbals public bar, charged with riding along the pavement on a velocipede to the obstruction of the passage, and with having, by so doing, thrown over a child."

On reaching the Barony of Gorbals, he had "gone upon the pavement, and was soon surrounded by a large crowd, attracted by the novelty of the machine.

"The child who was thrown down had not sustained any injury, and under the circumstances, the offender was fined only 5 shillings.

"The velocipede employed . . was very ingeniously constructed. It moved on wheels, turned by means of a crank; but to make it 'progress' appeared to require more labour than will be compensated for by the increase of speed."

The douce citizens of Glasgow were given a final assurance by the journalist who compiled the report. The Dumfriesshire gentleman's devilish invention, it was stated, would "not supersede the railway."

*   *   *

Although I have no documentary evidence to prove it, I somehow get the feeling that poor Macmillan was a bit non-plussed by all the excitement and fuss which his arrival had caused. Not to say embarrassed, too.

The news of his velocipede — "It actually goes by pedals without touching the ground!" — spread throughout the city, and everywhere the blacksmith went, he found himself surrounded by larger and more curious crowds. Everyone was intrigued by his new type of road machine.

It is not surprising that he stayed only for a brief period in the city, despite having two brothers living and working there.

As his son was later to tell me, the stir which his father had created proved a little too much for him., His only aim now, having proved that a man could go on two wheels, was to return to the green, pleasant and quiet fields around Courthill and Thornhill.

Village life, he decided, was infinitely preferable to the hubbub of the city.

So, two days later, Kirkpatrick said good-bye to his two brothers, John and George, and prepared to set off for home.

He didn't reckon on a little bit more excitement·on the return trip. As he left the city, astride the history-making machine, he encountered an acquaintance from his coachman days, one of the drivers of the Glasgow-Carlisle mail-coach.

The competition was too enticing to decline. "A'll lay you a wager, Jock," said Pate. "A'll wager you that A'll give you a square run for your money all the way back to Sanquhar, and that this velocipede of mine will make the journey faster than your own coach and horses."

"It's a deal!" said the coach driver. "Let's go!"

And that is why, down the road from Glasgow to Kilmarnock, speeding once again out of the city, went "Daft Pate" Macmillan on the world's first pedal bicycle, closely followed by Jock Davidson and the Carlisle mail-coach.

It was, as you will gather, a neck-and-neck race for many of the early miles, but Macmillan had the advantage of not having to halt and pick up country passengers at halts along the way, like his coachman colleague.

By the time he rode into Old Cumnock again, Macmillan had outstripped the coach, which was already lagging several miles behind. He rode, a fairly easy winner, into the village of Sanquhar sixty minutes after dusk that evening late in the June of 1842.

The onward journey from Sanquhar to Thornhill, and westwards the last few miles to Penpont and Courthill, was an easy one, and a tremendous welcome awaited the young son of the 'smithy when he finally reached home.

The news had spread all along the route that he was on his way back from Glasgow, and the country folk were on the watch for his approach.

Coming home after you have proved something is often so very different in reaction to when you leave. A prophet is usually minus honour in his own country, and neighbours and friends will scoff until you are proved a winner else-where. That's the way of this strange old world, and it was ever so, even in 1842.

The cries around Courthill smithy as the two-wheeled wanderer returned were in similar vein.

"Good auld Pate!", "Aye, you've shown them, laddie!", "Fame and fortune at last, Pate!", "You've made a right royal stir, Macmillan!"

These and other congratulations were the order of the June evening all along the final few miles of his journey from Thornhill to Keir. The prophet was at last being honoured — and in his ain countryside.

His former colleague John Findlater was at Courthill to greet Pate. So, of course, were his parents, Robert and Mary, and the other members of the blacksmith's family. All were proud that the lad had made such a name for himself up in the big city.

Now they realised that he wasn't really so "daft" after all, for he had made a machine to benefit humanity.

HOME AGAIN

East, West . . . and, as they say, home's best! So it was for Macmillan in the weeks and months following his history-making journey to Glasgow.

The youthful blacksmith had second thoughts on his new-found fame or notoriety, call it what you will. He had gained a new appreciation of the quiet country life to which he and most of his family were accustomed over the years.

Within a few weeks he had happily settled down once again to the blacksmith's life. He still took a great interest in his velocipede, of course, but friends noticed that he was not seen so often riding on it around the district.

Maybe he was slightly ashamed of having created so much consternation and, above all, of having been thrown into the public cells.

In the evenings, however, 'Pate' would work on his machine with renewed enthusiasm, improving a piece of mechanism here and there. He was certain it could be made more efficient. One device he adopted was to hollow out the horse's head at the front and convert it into a kind of receptacle for luggage.

Meanwhile, in other parts of Scotland, the news of the Dumfriesshire lad's now notorious pedal-propelled "horse" got quickly around. Copies of his machine were being constructed in various counties, and Macmillan's invention became the copyright of all.

There were other matters to keep Macmillan busy. The times were controversial, and in the days preceding the Disruption of 1843 he went over to the Seceders and changed his church to Virginhall, a mile and a half from Thornhill.

One is seldom bored in the country, and rural matters occupied much of his time.

He was a sort of acknowledged local veterinary surgeon, and was called on to attend to farmers' cows and horses for miles around. With his flair for working with horses he was naturally much in demand.

On the kitchen shelf at Courthill stood a large bottle, not unlike those we used to see inside the windows of confectionery shops in Scottish villages. But this was a bottle with a difference. It was nearly always filled with teeth, of both horses and humans, which Macmillan had pulled for friends, neighbours and customers.

There was a good social life around Keir Mill and Penpont. At weddings and dances the young blacksmith was keenly sought after, for he had a fair aptitude for whistling, and he played the violin better than most.

His craftsmanship as a blacksmith improved with the years, and he became one of the quickest in the parish at fashioning any article he was called upon to make.

In his work he was quick and thorough, and not afraid to put all his heart and soul and strength into it.

The big world outside could go by for all he cared. This was his life, that of a country blacksmith, and he wanted no more than to stay a useful craftsman and serve the country folk among whom he lived.

As 'Pate' was often heard to remark, the world outside could have his velocipede.

He, at least, had started the whole idea and invented pedal-propulsion, and there was no one who would dispute that fact. He had done something to give pleasure and recreation to millions, and a new sport to humanity.

Certainly Macmillan did appreciate that his pedal velocipede incorporated an intrinsically new idea. What he did not fully realise was that it was to mark the first step in the great and continuing development of the bicycle, down through the "penny-farthing" days to the modern lightweight of today.

So it came as a surprise to young 'Pate' when a letter arrived at Courthill 'smithy about six months after his trip to Glasgow, asking if he would consider an offer to work in a well-known Glasgow foundry.

"We were considerably impressed by the brief view we had of your pedal-driven velocipede," wrote the owner, "and, with your obvious ability for iron-working and your flair for thinking up new ideas, we should be happy to have you with us in a purely advisory capacity."

The wages offered Macmillan were good, and Kirkpatrick decided, there and then, to think it over and eventually accept the job. It would, he told himself, be valuable experience, and there was no knowing where this particular opportunity might lead.

There were difficulties in the way, however. 'Pate' could not accept immediately, for his father was not in the best of health, and he was duty bound to carry on at the Courthill anvil.

Work was flowing in to the smithy in greater quantities than ever before, and it seems as if every farmer and ploughman and cottager in the district wanted the Macmillan trademark on his repairs.

Meanwhile, something happened in the summer of 1844 that brought much pleasure to Macmillan.

A servant from the Buccleuch family estate at Drumlanrig called at Courthill with an invitation. The Dowager Duchess of Buccleuch, he said, was holding a garden party in the grounds of the castle, and some of the fine ladies and gentlemen of the county were going to be present.

Would Mr. Kirkpatrick Macmillan be so kind as to bring his famous and amusing velocipede up to the lawn that afternoon, and give a display for the benefit of the guests?

Would he! Wouldn't he just! The inventor was only too delighted to accept this opportunity of entertaining and edifying the fine people up at the Castle.

The occasion, it seems, proved a success, and Macmillan's prowess in steering and riding his machine in figures-of-eight around the lawn was warmly cheered.

So it wasn't until the Spring of 1845 that he eventually found the time to get away to his new situation in the Glasgow foundry.

He made the journey to the city by his velocipede again, but this time there was an absence of the stir which had marked his trip three years earlier.

People were still curious about the machine, but news of its arrival into the world had cooled down, although coopers and joiners and engineers in many counties were trying desperately to construct similar models from rough sketches of Macmillan's protoype.

The Scot from the quiet hamlet in Dumfriesshire had started something quite significant in the mid-40s of last century. And the world and his wife were soon to get down to the fascinating habit of riding around on a couple of wheels.

TO GLASGOW — RETURN RIDE

Macmillan's second journey by velocipede to Glasgow was made in 1845, three years after his pioneer run, and while it created much interest along the way, the excitement was as nothing compared to his epoch-making trip of June 1842.

But this time more and more people were interested in the potential of his cumbersome contrivance, and, with an eye on the main chance, not a few were anxious to find how they might capitalise on it.

One of these was Thomas McCall, joiner and wheelwright, of 1 High Street, Kilmarnock.

On that May morning in 1845 when "Daft Pate" rode past, McCall was standing outside his shop. The previous evening, as on the first occasion, Macmillan had arrived in Old Cumnock and had stayed once again with his friend, John McKinnell.

McCall had heard much talk of the Macmillan machine, and he took a closer look as the inventor rode by, even following it hotfoot for a short distance. There was a small fortune, he realised, to be made in turning out contrivances like this and in large numbers.

As he somewhat warily rode into Glasgow on that May late afternoon in 1845, the blacksmith was welcomed with open arms by the engineers and the business gentlemen of the city. There was not the same alarm as in the June of 1842.

The commercially-minded types of the city on the Clyde knew now that, in this inventive countryman, they had located a Scot with a genius for new ideas, and it was these very new ideas that were wanted and needed in the changing industrial era they lived in.

Macmillan found useful work to do at the foundry where his new job was.

One of his workmates was a certain James Thomson who came from Blantyre, outside Glasgow, and Macmillan spent several worthwhile weekends at his city lodgings at 94 Thistle Street, on the south side of the Clyde.

One night at Thomson's residence they got into conversation with William Thomson, a brother, who came from Auchinraith, Blantyre.

"You know, James," said 'Pate', stretching himself before a comfortable fire, "you know, I never dreamt for one minute when I started all this ploy that the thing would have such tremendous results. It has well and truly mushroomed."

In the next hour Macmillan kept his city-based listeners entranced and amazed with tales of his adventures on country roads and byways as the world's first man-on-two-wheels.

He told them of the stubborn opposition to his idea, mainly by friends and neighbours at home in Dumfriesshire.

He told them of the famous ride to Glasgow from Courthill in June 1842, of his appearance before the magistrate in the Gorbals police court . . . and of dozens of other difficulties and problems that had confronted him in the making of the velocipede.

'Pate', a handsome and tall Scot, reminisced over his experiences.

"Aye, man," he smiled, "It's getting to be a real craze now. If you haven't got one of these road machines today, then you'll just not be in the fashion at all!

"D'ye ken who asked to buy one from me a month ago? Aye, none other than the Duke o' Buccleuch himsel', and he wasn't sparing wi' the money, either.

"I'd already made him one as a present, and was he delighted! Asked me tae come over and see him, and there and then he ordered another.

" 'Pate', says he, 'I think you've got somethin' here.'

" 'Your Grace', says I, 'I thank you kindly for the compliment. I never thought for one minute that my idea would have such an effect. I thank you kindly, sir.' "

Macmillan, alas, was too friendly and outgoing a countryman to keep his secret trade techniques to himself.

If he had been a more astute young fellow in a business sense, he would, I'm sure, have kept his invention to himself, guarded it even more closely, and probably made a fortune from it.

But, being the friendly Scot he was, he did not believe in keeping things to himself.

Friends and neighbours, and even chance acquaintances, who expressed a desire for a pedal steed had only to ask him — and, hey presto, Macmillan would build them one.

Little wonder, then, that blacksmiths and coopers and craftsmen in different parts of Scotland were turning copyists and reproducing his velocipede.

Thomas McCall, the Kilmarnock joiner and wheel-wright, who had watched him ride by to Glasgow, built — and sold — more than a dozen copies at £7 each. He made his first one by purchasing John Findlater's old dandy-horse for five shillings and attaching driving gear.

Word of the two-wheeled wonder machine with cranks spread south of Gretna Green, and people in the south of England were soon sending orders to McCall. One came from an English country doctor, and this, in turn, was re-copied considerably over a wide area.

For Macmillan the rural life was beckoning again, and he did not tarry long in the city foundry. His father had taken ill again, the work was piling up at the family smithy, and the pleasant country life was proving too strong a magnet.

Which is why, in the autumn of 1845, we find him riding home again. His idea was already benefiting humanity, and 'Pate' was content to let it be that way.

A GOOD IDEA, SON . . .!

There are too few good ideas in the world. A bit of inventiveness, and you can be a winner.

As they always say, grab a good and novel idea, one that will help people to a better life, and the world will beat a path to your door.

Alas, it wasn't the smithy door in quiet Keir Mill, Dumfriesshire, to which the world's velocipede-makers came, as well they ought.

Instead, go-ahead craftsmen were already cashing-in on the Macmillan idea, and another was George McCartney, who owned a millwright and engineer's works in Old Cumnock and who had seen 'Daft Pate' pass through the village on that historic ride of 1842.

Yet another was Gavin Dalzell, a cooper and merchant in Lesmahagow, who became so well-known for turning out crank-driven velocipedes that, for some years afterwards, he was acknowledged as the inventor of the geared dandy-horse.

By a strange irony, if Macmillan had not chosen to vary his homeward route from Glasgow in 1845, Dalzell would probably never have been able to "steal his thunder."

As it happened, of course, the Dumfriesshire blacksmith decided, for a change, to take the Hamilton and Lesmahagow road, and to ride home by way of Abington, Elvanfoot, the Dalveen Pass and Carronbridge.

Gavin Dalzell was going his rounds one day in 1845 when he saw Macmillan ride past. He had just time to spy out how the famous velocipede was constructed.

The man from Lesmahagow had a retentive memory, and when he got home that evening, he immediately made a rough sketch of the contrivance.

Then he set to work, and within a few months had constructed a machine which, in appearance, was an almost exact replica of the original Macmillan rear-driven model.

According to my information, Dalzell's machine was built mainly of wood. Its rear wheel, shod with iron, was about forty inches in diameter, and had twelve spokes, each about an inch in diameter.

His front wheel was of a similar construction, but of only some 30 inches in diameter.

We know that the local blacksmith, one John Leslie, of Lesmahagow, made all the ironwork for Gavin Dalzell. By the summer of 1846 his velocipede was ready for the road.

Since he lived so close to the growing industrialised central belt of Scotland, Dalzell was able to let his machine be viewed by probably more people and over a longer period than Macmillan had ever done.

In fact, people kept coming to him and asked how they might build one.

Unselfishly, he showed them, and in the years from 1846 to 1850 many similar velocipedes, with pedal propulsion, came into use in different parts of Scotland.

One typical order was from Francis Forrest, living at Carnwath, in Lanarkshire.

In November 1848, he wrote to Dalzell;

"Sir — As I did not see you when I was down to get a full account of your riding machine at that time, if you would be so good as to write me all about it, say what you rate you can go a mile easily up hill, and if you would make on this draft the lengths of the different parts, you will oblige me."

Having launched his idea upon an unsuspecting and, I fear, a rather sneering and suspicious world, Macmillan was already relinquishing his role of the world's pioneer bicycle rider and turning to being a blacksmith again.

He became, in fact, something of a forgotten man while credit for inventing the bicycle stayed for a dozen years or so with Gavin Dalzell, of Lesmahagow.

It was not until about the year 1888 that James Johnston, of the Glasgow Tri-cycling Club, having a pretty strong idea that Macmillan was the real inventor, set on foot a series of investigations.

Johnston, a keen cyclist, travelled many miles to confirm his facts and wrote hundreds of letters.

For his main piece of evidence he pulled in a large number of living witnesses who had frequently seen and known Macmillan.

By great good fortune one of his informants was John Findlater, blacksmith, of Carronbridge — the same John Findlater who had been a workmate of Macmillan in his youth.

Scores of other people gave valuable evidence and contributed many valuable reminiscnces of seeing the inventor on various dates during his career.

An Old Cumnock native was able to tell the story of 'Pate's' midnight ride down McKinlay's Brae into the village and to name the young shoemaker who had taken to his heels in fright at the sight of the "Devil on Wheels."

Thereby lies a romantic tale, for it was known that this young shoemaker, one James Kennedy, had married the girl he had been escorting home on that historic night only a few months after the Macmillan incident.

Kennedy's daughter was traced to her home in Ayrshire, and his marriage certificate was produced.

This proclaimed that "James Kennedy and Jean Vallance" were married at Cumnock on the 19th day of August, 1842."

John McKinnell, the schoolmaster — with whom Macmillan had lodged for the night on his 1842 journey — had himself signed their marriage proclamation in his capacity as Session Clerk to the Parish Church.

Final proof that Macmillan was the first man ever to ride a bicycle came when a search was made of old newspaper files, and the historic Court report, describing his appearance at the Gorbals Public Bar, was discovered.

After the era of the direct-driven high "ordinary" or "penny-farthing", the machine most folk associate with early bicycles, came something more approaching the modern lightweight bicycle of today.

It is a far cry from the cumbersome 57 lbs wood-and-iron machine that 'Pate' Macmillan built, but it is really not that much changed in construction, except for its chain-driven propulsion and its rotary-motion pedals.

Just what happened to Kirkpatrick Macmillan, his life and career — and to the bicycle craze between the mid-1860s and today — I shall leave to my closing chapters. Suffice to say that this inventive countryman from the Scottish Lowlands did not languish into obscurity, but became a couthy character of his district, and a man the ladies came to admire and love.

A RURAL MAN O' PAIRTS

Away from his blacksmith's "smithy" and the demanding task of constructing velocipedes for Jock Tamson and his brood, Kirkpatrick Macmillan was a typical Scottish countryman of the 19th century, a man who could turn his hands to many a trade and who made the most of his private life.

Like most Scots in the rural backwoods of the Scottish Lowlands, he had great faith, was extremely devout, and a loyal churchman. With his two offspring, Mary and John, he walked each Sabbath morning to Virginhall Free Church, and they sat in the back pew in the gallery.

By nature this "mad" inventor was a mild-tempered soul, sympathetic and kind-hearted.

The country folk with whom I talked in the course of my researches told me how, from their own parents, they heard of the hospitality and kindness that was part of the family at Courthill.

Never, they said, was a tramp or travelling pedlar turned away from the door without being given something to eat and drink.

Religious he was to an intense degree, Kirkpatrick Macmillan. The wintry elements put them on their mettle, and whenever the nearby River Scaur overflowed its banks, Macmillan would call his family indoors, take down the family Bible — and each of them would read a chapter.

All through his life, from lively boyhood to a maturer middle age, Macmillan retained a kindly humour and a boyish sense of fun. He exuded an infectious spirit of gaiety that was loved by all with whom he came in contact.

Life had probably not been as kind as it might have been to the Keir blacksmith, but he had made the most of it, and he did not regret one minute of the passing years.

He was, of course, a Scotsman of very high principles. Against drink and tobacco he was extremely bitter, and many a time he would offer his smithy apprentices a two-shilling piece if they would promise to stop smoking.

His son, John Macmillan, was able to confirm this trait when I met him.

One day his father asked John, then a young lad, for a piece of slate pencil.

John remembered how he put his hand into his waist-coat pocket — all boys in Scotland sported waistcoats in that era — and handed a bit to his father.

But 'Pate', after using it, happened to put it into his mouth, and a look of stern-ness and anger came over his kindly face. He had tasted the nasty tobacco on it!

He made a grab at his son, chased him out of the smithy, called him a lazy good-for-nothing, and ordered him to go and hire for the harvest.

*   *   *

Children did not always survive into youth and middle-age in 19th century Scotland. Hospitals and physicians had little of the expertise of today, and mortality among growing families — and especially babies — was high. The family at Courthill did not escape.

Mary Lillias, first child born to Kirkpatrick and his wife Elspeth, died in the June of 1856, at the age of 14 months. A year later a second daughter, Annie Christina, died at 10 months.

Two more of their offsping died some time later, one named Kirkpatrick after his father, the other Robert after his grandfather. So, finally, only two were left — John Macmillan, later to be resident in Liverpool, and Mary, who became a teacher.

'Pate's' mother, Mary, died, we know, in the July of 1860 at the age of 77, and — his father already dead — Courthill and its busy smithy was left totally in the capable charge of Kirkpatrick and his wife Elspeth.

Robert Macmillan, father of the family, and himself no less a respected figure than his son 'Pate', had taken ill in the winter of 1853 when his inventor son reached his 40th birth-day. He died at home on the fourth of February in the following year — at the age of 75.

It was around this time that Macmillan, now the master of Courthill, took a special think to himself and decided it was high time he settled down and took a wife.

Until now he had been given little time or opportunity to think of marriage.

The story of how he met and proposed to his future wife is a curious one.

He was called over one day to do some work to the horses for the Arundell family at Barjarg Towers, in the south end of Keir Parish.

According to all reports, 'Pate' finished his task and was invited into the kitchen for a mug of tea.

Some half-dozen servant girls were busy preparing the evening meal for the Arundell family.

If truth be told, more than one of them had thought of the handsome Courthill village blacksmith as a possible husband, but it appeared to all and sundry that he was resigned to his work, to building velocipedes, and to staying a bachelor.

Macmillan, as I have said, was always fond of perpetrating a joke, and they say — and there is no reason to disbelieve the story — that he strode jauntily into the Barjarg kitchen on that afternoon in the spring of 1854 and smiled at the lassies of the household, then — suddenly and as if by impulse — blurted out, in a semi-jocular tone:

"Say, lassies, is there ony yin here that'll mak' a guid wife tae me?"

Naturally, the servant lassies were taken aback. They well knew 'Pate' Macmillan's fondness for a joke, but this time they detected just a shade of serious intent behind the blacksmith's smile.

One of the girls, pretty Elspeth Gordon Goldie, knew, almost instinctively, that this was her chance.

She was still only 21, but she was a lady's maid, and she rather liked the tall good-looking blacksmith, although she well realised he was at least twice her age.

Blushingly, she stepped forward, looked up at Kirkpatrick, and, in a quiet voice, said simply: "I will!"

An odd proposal indeed, but a genuine one. And a genuine acceptance.

A few weeks later 'Pate' and Elspeth became engaged. Before the year was out, they had travelled to Edinburgh and been pronounced man and wife.

THE QUIET LIFE

Kirkpatrick Macmillan did little riding on his historic velocipede in his latter years. Happily married, he preferred home life and the quiet of a country community.

We do know that he tried out the new "boneshaker" type of bicycle, driven by cranks direct on to the axle of the front wheel, but he never really mastered this, as he had done with his own invention.

In fact, it looked now as if the world was beginning to forget that he was, indeed, the original inventor.

Down in Coventry, in the English Midlands, the Lion Bicycle Company were offering the Macmillan type for sale and, in their advertisements, were calling it the "Dalzell Bicycle".

'Pate' still rode this bicycle along the quiet Dumfriesshire roads and lanes, but all his enthusiasm for the sport appeared to have gone. And it seemed ages now since that historic June evening when he had set off for Glasgow in 1842.

From time to time young people would ask Macmillan about his velocipede, and he would regain some of his old keen-ness. Especially when his niece, Mary Marchbank, would coax him to give her a spin on it down the roadway to Penpont village.

Mary was the daughter of Isabella Macmillan, who had lived at Moniaive when he was building his machine, and who later married George Marchbank, one-time precentor in the parish church at Closeburn.

Mary felt quite a daring young lady as she sat perched on Uncle 'Pate's' shoulders and went gliding down to the village where her school-mates lived.

Meanwhile, at Courthill smithy, the Macmillan family heard little news of the development of the bicycle in the far corners of Britain and the world.

Sometimes, of an evening, 'Pate' would draw in the chairs round the fireside, and, round the glowing embers, tell an entrancing tale or two of his pioneer trips and his ride to the city. But of what was going on in other places he knew little.

Elspeth, his wife, did not keep in the best of health. Doctors were called in but, despite their efforts, she grew worse of the fever and died on the 28th of July, 1865. She was only 32.

Only the two remaining children, John and Mary, and Aunt Ann ('Pate's' sister) and the little niece Mary Marchbank were left to comfort the Keir blacksmith for his remaining years.

Aunt Ann kept house for the family and for Kirkpatrick, now in his 52nd year.

*   *   *

It was around this period that Macmillan turned his attention to the farm plough and succeeded in devising a number of improvements.

He made two machines that differed from the ordinary plough, and exhibited one of them at the Highland Agricultural Show at Dumfries.

Instead of the two sides running up from the body to the handle, he built one single bar and had handles fastened on the end after the fashion of modern bicycle handlebars.

On the old plough the part at the front end where the swingletrees were fastened on by a cleek had to be shifted from one end to the other by a pin, and the horses had to be un-yoked before the pin could be shifted. Macmillan made this link to be shifted by a screw so that there was no need to uncouple the swingletrees.

A favourite remark by Macmillan about this new plough was to the effect that "it could be taken to pieces and put in a chest".

He also made a number of farming implements for the great Mr Gladstone, at that time Chancellor of the Exchequer, and he was proud of a letter he received from him complimenting him on his work.

*   *   *

Inside the Dumfriesshire smithy the original Macmillan velocipede still lay, but few if any of those who passed by, or looked inside, realised that one day, if it were preserved, this rickety piece of wood and iron would have a value that could not be easily assessed.

The story goes that 'Pate' was seated by the fireside after supper one night when a neighbour brought in an English periodical which he had acquired from a traveller passing through Thornhill.

It was "The English Mechanic", and it was dated June, 1869.

'Pate' turned the pages and stopped at an advertisement inside.

The bicycle, it seemed, was still being popularised, and a firm in the English Midlands were offering what they termed "The Kilmarnock Bicycle" at a cost of £7.

Macmillan must have had a quiet smile to himself. So they were crediting the Ayrshire town with the invention nowadays!

What he did not know was that others were cashing-in steadily on his original idea, and that Thomas McCall, the joiner and wheelwright he had heard of, was bringing in a goodly number of £7 fees for his copies of the Macmillan velocipede.

THE WORLD MUST REMEMBER. . .

If you go — by bicycle, car or on foot — to the old kirk-yard in Keir Mill, Dumfriesshire, spare ten minutes, I beg you, to visit the family grave of the Macmillans.

There, you will read, that "the above Kirkpatrick Macmillan, . . died at Courthill, Keir, 26th January 1878, aged 65 years."

At the foot of the tombstone are the four simple words —

"Inventor of the Bicycle."

Few folk know of this grave. Or of its significance. Cyclists arrive from England and from Germany, Holland and Belgium, to pay their respects.

It is ironical, I feel, that so few Scots, if any, ever call at Keir Mill or the Courthill smithy — or even know of this grave, surely a cyclists' shrine for all time.

When 'Daft Pate' died — and by now the epithet 'daft' had almost been forgotten — the news was a shock to the people in his parish who had come to know and respect the clever, kenspeckle blacksmith of Keir.

Hundreds, we know, turned out from near and far to follow his coffin to the auld kirkyard in Keir, close to the gurgling Scaur Water he had known so well.

But the world, as always, was inclined to forget that this Scot was the true inventor of the pedal-driven bicycle.

After his death the rear-driven bicycle came into fashion again, and then, for a short time, John Citizen and his wife went to town on the old direct-driven high "ordinary" or "penny-farthing."

It was, of course, a passing phase. The ladies of the naughty '90s were stoned for daring to disport and debase themselves by riding before the public gaze!

But, of course, the bicycle craze went on, and today the modern lightweight machine is with us, a far cry from the era of that 57 lb. wood-and-iron contraption that a daft laddie from southern Scotland built and rode on in the 1840's.

Look closely, however, at today's bicycles. They are not greatly changed in construction, except for the chain-driven propulsion and the rotary motion pedals.

In the war against Hitler, when austerity prevailed and motor-cars had no petrol for pleasure-driving, men and women all round the world went back to . . . yes, the humble, the simple bicycle. The machine that 'Pate' built has proved its worth in every age and clime.

It is surely only right that today the whole world should remember Macmillan. Britain's cycle manufacturers and cyclists owe a debt to the man who showed us how to get around on two wheels, not four.

In the Springtime days of 1946, British cycling enthusiasts made a pilgrimmage to the smithy at Courthill to honour the bicycle inventor at a simple ceremony at which Sir Harold Bowden, Chairman of the National Committee on Cycling, unveiled a plaque in tribute.

But what ever became of Macmillan's original velocipede? All of us would dearly love to know.

They say in his home territory that the original velocipede was sold to a country pedlar and broken up for scrap. Its fate is still a mystery.

Only replicas remain — in the Burgh Museum at Dumfries, in Glasgow's Transport Museum, and in the South Kensington Museum in London.

It is odd to think, today, that the Romans never thought of the bicycle. If they had put two wheels together, they might have come invading Britain on velocipedes, not in chariots.

Back in 1790 a French count, the Comte de Sivrac, rode around the Palais-Royal garden in Paris on a wooden bar attached to two wheels, propelling himself with his feet. That was the "dandy-horse." In 1819 a coachbuilder in Long Acre, London, started building them. But it was not until 20 years later that Macmillan of Scotland had a better idea — pedal propulsion.

The 1890s and the 1900s were the golden age of the bicycle, and it is a pity, I always think, that Macmillan did not live to see his idea take full shape.

Riding bicycles is big on the Continent of Europe. They say the whole population of Holland, a land of flat terrain, could go for a bicycle ride at the same time. Half of the eleven million folk in the Netherlands own bicycles.

They say it is no harder to ride a bicycle than it is to walk, but it goes four or five times as fast. And, down-hill, you don't need any leg power.

In Britain alone, at a recent count, more than sixteen-million bicycles were being used on the roads.

Every year Britain produces nearly two million bicycles. Of that total, 900, 000 are sold overseas and to developing countries.

Scots may regret that the original Kirkpatrick Macmillan bicycle is no longer extant, but surely the great-est tribute to the invention is with us yet.

You find it on any road or street in city, town or countryside, in every corner of the world — a man or a woman, a boy or a girl, riding a bicycle.

I wonder how many of them know just how much they owe to a "mad" blacksmith from a quiet parish in southern Scotland, name of Kirkpatrick Macmillan, who devised the first pedal-driven machine.

For that reason, surely, he deserves the thanks of humanity, and to be better known than he is.

"DAFT PATE" and his Family.

Period photographs tell the story

If you come across a 19th-century photograph album, examine it closely. It could be worth its weight in gold!

The authentic family album and other photographs and drawings I have been able to unearth concerning the bicycle inventor, his home and relatives, are a lucky find.

For, in the now-faraway days of last century, especially in a rural corner of Scotland, good photographs were the exception.

I was fortunate to be loaned some by country folk around Thornhill village, in Dumfriesshire. Others I collected through the good offices of members of the Macmillan clan, now scattered far and wide from Scotland to Australia and North America.

The value of such pictorial memorabilia as I have been able to locate is considerable, however.

The photographs and other authentic evidence you see in the following pages is enough to remind us that — for all the romance surrounding his true-life story — Macmillan from Courthill, in Dumfriesshire, was a real person, a Scotsman who deserves well his place in the lengthy line of inventors who sprang from the Scottish Highlands and Lowlands.

Macmillan —
a period photograph.

Courthill Smithy — where it all began.

'Pate', his wife and son John.

Thornhill, close to Macmillan's home hamlet of Keir Mill.

Courthill Smithy
(Photo —
R.M. Pepper)

IN THIS SMITHY
THE FIRST BICYCLE
WAS BUILT BY THE
INVENTOR

KIRKPATRICK McMILLAN
ABOUT THE YEAR
1840

Plaque -
on the
smithy wall

Remembered — Centenary Year Plaque at Courthill, Dumfriesshire.

Replica of Macmillan's velocipede.

died 1st Nov.r 1865, aged 6 years. Also,
the above Kirkpatrick Macmillan, who died
at Courthill Keir, 26th Jan.y 1878, aged 65 years.
Inventor of the Bicycle.

Family grave — at cemetery in Keir Mill, Dumfriesshire.

One of Macmillan's apprentices made this velocipede about 1860.
(Photo — Thomson, blacksmith, Thornhill)